Amla Spe

Amla Mehta

Green Heart Living Press

ISBN Paperback: 978-1-954493-14-8

Cover photo credit: Amy Lyn Sundgren with specials thanks to S.M.

This book is designed to provide information and motivation to our readers. It is sold with the understanding that the publisher is not engaged to render any type of psychological, legal, or any other kind of professional advice. The content of each article is the sole expression and opinion of its author, and not necessarily that of the publisher. No warranties or guarantees are expressed or implied by the publisher's choice to include any of the content in this volume. Neither the publisher nor the individual author(s) shall be liable for any physical, psychological, emotional, financial, or commercial damages, including, but not limited to, special, incidental, consequential or other damages. Our views and rights are the same: You are responsible for your own choices, actions, and results.

This book is intended and designed for you to self-assess based on your outlook on life. Nobody is obligated to partake in the exercises/practices offered by Amla Mehta. Listen to your mind, body, spirit and inner-knowingness to decide if you wish to participate in these exercises.

Dedication

I would like to dedicate this book to the Creator, with thanks for granting me this blessed opportunity to express my insights based on my journey of spiritual ascension.

I also dedicate this book to my parents and sister. I love you! And to all beings who are facing difficult and challenging times. Please reach out to me if you need any heartfelt support.

I would also like to dedicate this book to all of my family and friends who have encouraged me to keep writing and share my wisdom no matter how challenging life can be.

Last, I would like to dedicate this book to you, dear reader. Without you, I would not be able to be seen, be heard, or share my inner knowingness. Thank you!

Introduction

Let's imagine we are all scuba divers in the middle of the deep blue ocean where nobody compares themselves with one another, including the shade of blue water that we swim in. We are all "humans that are being," united and living as one.

If we, as a collective community, are all swimming in the same ocean, maybe, just maybe, we can accept one another unconditionally with kindness and compassion.

More importantly, there is no judgment if my goal is to dive to 1,000 feet while another person chooses to dive to 200 feet. The thousand-foot diver might plunge in, knowing the murkier the waters become the more hardships they must navigate while descending to the ocean's floor. At the same time, on this fascinating journey of wonder, there could be incredible sights and sounds to absorb, including colorful fish and coral reefs.

Diving into the unknown waters may cause more wear and tear on the mind, body, and spirit; however, the decision is ours as to how we adapt and swim through this magical abyss. Whatever depth one chooses, there can be a sense of purpose to thrive and persevere. Again, whether our goal is 200 feet or 1,000 feet, if we set out on our destination with great drive and determination it is possible to achieve our ultimate goal. Life is not a competition; showing up and being our best is enough. We must focus on our own diving skills, and not be concerned by the other divers around us. After all, each of us can only breathe and live for ourselves.

The further we maneuver our way through the muck and guck layers of the seas the more likely we are to reach the one-of-a-kind finds that lay at the bottom of the ocean floor desperately waiting to be discovered. We must take a chance to challenge ourselves and go deeper than we ever could've imagined to find the priceless trinkets and treasures we've been yearning for.

As I face gyrate atrophy, an eye condition that causes gradual vision loss, I won't fully grasp the reality of being sightless until I've reached that state – much like the anticipation of the advanced swimming skills needed to be an expert scuba diver.

Despite the unpredictable changes in life, no matter what types of challenges emerge, it's our choice how we, as a society, respond and impact the world using the basic five senses (sight, sound, smell, taste, and touch) along with the sixth sense, known as the third eye, representing our intuition.

Despite my living with less physical eyesight, I have gained tremendous insight using my third eye as my "real eyes" to see and feel with heartfelt passion and purpose within the core layers of my being. More importantly, the impending vision loss represents a major reason to connect with my guiding light and pure love straight from the heart, without any external visual distractions.

Whether I like it or not, my life has and will be forever changed as my eyesight gradually decreases. However, living in the present gives me more reason to value each and every moment with child-like innocence and curiosity.

Given the uncertainty of the pandemic ravaging our society, people are constantly asking, "When is this pandemic going to end?" Sooner or later, this too shall pass, and we, as human beings, shall rise above to become greater, wiser, and stronger. I must, we must, hold onto hope, and find new and innovative ways to soar through life and embrace the infinite possibilities of feeling and being unconditional love.

Whatever our circumstances may withhold, in good times and bad times, life is encompassed with many shades of lightness and darkness.

Through this collection of insights and reflections, it is my desire to share my unique world with my real eyes that see from the heart. Because while I am losing my physical vision, I'll never lose my eternal vision of unconditional love and unity for all of mankind.

Amla Mehta

Reflection 1
Wisdom
Thoughts and emotions are like ocean waves, drifting in and out of consciousness. It's up to you what you do with the waves of life.

Reflection 2
Authenticity
Love accepts you just the way you are. Why don't you?

Reflection 3
Setting Healthy Boundaries
When I ask for help, just respond with a "yes" or "no." It's a win-win situation for both parties. I respect your honesty while you set forth strong and healthy boundaries.

Reflection 4
Wisdom
You must empathize with others to genuinely understand others.

Reflection 5
Mehta Mantra
I am powerful.
I am respectable.
I am honorable.
So it is.
(Repeat)

Reflection 6
Unconditional Love
When you wholeheartedly love yourself, there's nothing to prove, not even to yourself.

Reflection 7
Wisdom
Use your nurturing voice as an open vessel to take care of yourself.

Reflection 8
Wisdom
Meet your shadow parts in order to meet your lighter parts to find inner peace. The law of nature only works that way.

Reflection 9
Happiness
When you embrace aging through life, you enjoy the rainbow spectrum of life.

Reflection 10
Love
The key ingredient to be your authentic self is tapping into the purest form of yourself – unconditional love.

Reflection 11
Self-Love
Embellish your life with sweetness and kindness each and every day.

Reflection 12
Wisdom
Personal growth is an individual process. After all, not every first grader in school learns their addition skills at the same time. Value your own life path.

Reflection 13
Wisdom
Being whole is a sole and a soul "job."

Reflection 14
Standing in My Power
I am just as human as the person next to me.
With that, it's my birthright to be treated
equally.

Reflection 15
Self-Care Practice
All beings have hardships big and small. How
do you cope with the ups and downs of life?

Name three tangible things you do for your
self-care on a daily basis.

Reflection 16
The Art of Detachment
When you detach from something or someone, it doesn't imply for you to avoid, remain aloof, or be dismissive. Rather, detachment is about accepting the situation or person objectively, without any judgment or attachment, and, ultimately, walking away with a smile on your face.

Reflection 17
Authenticity
Short, tall, fat, small we are all one and original simultaneously.

Reflection 18
Optimism
Life is never boring when you're open and receptive to learning something new.

Reflection 19

Empowerment

Great leaders are exceptional at their work because they encourage their team to accept the wins with humility while accepting their falls as an opportunity for perseverance.

Reflection 20

Love and Nurture

The mother of the heart cares. The father of the heart knows. Both qualities are needed to live a well-balanced life.

Reflection 21
Mehta Mantra
I am calm.
I am capable.
I am one who is fully supported by the Higher
Power, God, Source, Creator.
So it is.
(Repeat)

Reflection 22
"One" Affirmation
I consciously accept all beings as
interconnected, unified, and living as one love.

Reflection 23
Wisdom
Be the significant reason you are in someone's
life, not for the sake of a short season.

Reflection 24
Wisdom
A wise person knows when and where to speak up, and also knows when and where to remain silent. Be wise with wide-open eyes.

Reflection 25
Wisdom
Although I cannot change my yesterday, I can choose to change my today.

Reflection 26
Pure Love Exercise
There are a number of ways to show a person you love them without spending any money. Name five things you could do to show somebody you unconditionally love them.

Reflection 27

Wisdom

Courage and inner strength are tested when you hit rock bottom, not when you're standing at the top.

Reflection 28

Amla's Insight

By facing numerous roller coaster rides of emotional turmoil, trials, and tribulations, I have found trust and faith for my own self-preservation.

Reflection 29
Self-Fulfillment Practice
Without hurts and wounds, there's no opportunity for hope and healing. Start by tapping into your authentic self.

Name five intangible qualities you love about yourself.

Reflection 30
Letting Go Practice
There are three key components to surrender.
1. Set the intention from the heartspace not the headspace.
2. Allow what is transpiring to unfold organically.
3. Trust the process.

How do you choose to let go and surrender?

Reflection 31
Speaking Your Truth
I shift and sweep through my life in my time,
not anybody else's projected timeline.

Reflection 32
Being Present
When I feel like I am inundated with
unforeseen change, I remember that
everything is temporary and that each
moment is old and new simultaneously. Being
present is a priceless gift.

Reflection 33
Self-Full of Love Practice
Look into a mirror and place your hand on
your heart while gazing into your eyes.
Say, "I love you <your first name>," out loud.
(Repeat)
Aren't you worth the self-investment?

Reflection 34

Wisdom

Gravitate toward ascension by allowing things to unfold without needing to take hold.

Reflection 35

Wisdom

Old ways of thinking, behaving, and being cannot activate new and innovative ways of creating.

Reflection 36

Wisdom

Sometimes you have to move with the rushing waters of the river to get things flowing into motion.

Reflection 37
Authenticity
I make my mark on the world by being my spectacular self, reflecting my own self-expression.

Reflection 38
Inspiration
When your heart is filled with passion, your mind, will, and determination make anything happen.

Reflection 39
Trust and Faith
One must have faith for each breath one takes.

Reflection 40
Intuition
I see right through you with my eyes closed.

Reflection 41
Unconditional Love
The more I face and embrace my dark layers,
the more light and love illuminates through
me, infinitely.

Reflection 42
Mehta Mantra
I am patient.
I am determined.
I am worthy.
So it is.
(Repeat)

Reflection 43
I Surrender
Sometimes you have to speak your truth in totality in order to detach and let go fully.

Reflection 44
Authenticity
It's the irregularities and shimmery qualities that inspire me to sprinkle my luminous light everywhere I am.

Reflection 45
Setting Healthy Boundaries
Just because I need help doesn't mean I am incapable or needy.
A healthy relationship incorporates three fundamental components:
1. Independence
2. Dependence
3. Interdependence

Reflection 46
Amla's Insight
Through this process of losing my vision, it has become increasingly clear to me that everything revolves around the countless layers of illusion.

Reflection 47
Wisdom
Your heart represents the motor of your soul fueling you to elevate higher and higher throughout all directions of space and time.

Reflection 48
Wisdom
Letting go is a process. Embrace it, and when you are perfectly ready to surrender, all the good stuff pours in.

Reflection 49
Transformation
Change either makes you or breaks you. You define how it will affect you.

Reflection 50
Wisdom
Sometimes you just need to be heard and validated by somebody you care about.

Reflection 51
Resilience
My heart has been stomped on over and over again, but I also became stronger and wiser over and over again.

Reflection 52
Amla's Insight
The paintbrushes that I use symbolize speaking my truth. I love painting with my words.

Reflection 53
Wisdom
Sometimes the only way to fill yourself up is to realize your inner gauge is running empty.

Reflection 54
Happiness
Allow your heart to flourish without fearing what's next. Remember, everything happens for your ultimate bliss.

Reflection 55
Authenticity
Be your one-of-a-kind-self by connecting with your heart, while thinking for yourself, independently.

Reflection 56
Trust and Faith
Think of faith as a flicker of pinpoint light inside of you. Always remember that when you feel lost and alone, you can reconnect to the love and light from within.

Reflection 57
Wisdom
Don't allow others to hijack your thoughts and feelings. After all, you are the master of your own life.

Reflection 58
Wisdom
Just because you switch gears into reverse doesn't mean you're permanently heading in that direction. When a car is parked, the driver must shift into reverse in order to move forward.

Reflection 59
Wisdom
Life is short. Be selective and only subscribe to your soul tribe.

Reflection 60
Wisdom
To love wholeheartedly in the present, you must drain and empty out the pain from the past.

Reflection 61
Mehta Mantra
I am a piece of the divine naturally projecting peace out into the world.

Reflection 62
Amla's Insight
Living life with blurred vision, I have a crystal-clear view.

Reflection 63
Unconditional Love
Love like no other even when you find yourself stuck in a corner.

Reflection 64
Wisdom
The "child" of the relationship reacts and the "parent" of the relationship responds. For all intents and purposes, we all have our moments of portraying both archetypes within our relationships. When friction occurs, pause in the present moment, especially when you have the urge to react. With that, you're more likely to respond with grace and ease.

Reflection 65
Self-Love
Find love and support from within and, like a boomerang, love and support come right back to you.

Reflection 66
Wisdom
Life is like the game of poker. The universe deals you the cards. In the end, it's up to you whether or not you make a good hand out of the cards you are dealt.

Reflection 67
Wisdom
Let go of control and ego and allow the outcome to unveil itself naturally. It might not be what you expected, but more times than not, the learning process occurs in miraculous ways.

Reflection 68
Being Whole
There is no need to compete with yourself when you feel fully complete within yourself.

Reflection 69
Transformation
The choice is up to you to say "yes" and grow during an uncomfortable change or say "no" and stay the same.

Reflection 70
Wisdom
Without faith and trust in yourself there isn't a "trustworthy handshake" between you and the universe.

Reflection 71
Mehta Mantra
I am alive.
I do my best.
I am limitless.
So it is.
(Repeat)

Reflection 72
Wisdom
The real adventure in life is not about how many trips you've taken externally; it's the willingness to stretch far and wide, internally.

Reflection 73
Unconditional Love
I open my eyes to see my internal reflection of eternal love for myself.

Reflection 74
Amla's Insight
I cannot imagine a life without Creator, hope, and faith guiding me each and every day.

Reflection 75
Inspiration
I crave nothing but an eternity of beauty, bliss, and serenity through the endless fields of love while I dance to the rhythm of my own heartbeat.

Reflection 76
Trust and Faith
I allow myself to trust the road of spiritual success through endless times of glory, wit, and weariness.

Reflection 77
Amla's Revelation
I am standing up for the people who encounter and endure the strange beast of ignorance, indifference, and intolerance from society.

Reflection 78
Wisdom
I cannot determine who or where I will be at the year's end, but I do know I won't be the same.

Reflection 79
Wisdom
The heart never stumps you; it's your mind that bumps you along the path of life. Always listen and trust your heart.

Reflection 80
Acceptance
I take my time to adjust to change and uncertainty. Only then, can I graciously move on with poise and integrity.

Reflection 81
Standing in My Power
Against all odds, I am my own self-advocate.
Nobody else can do that for me.

Reflection 82
Wisdom
A 24-hour day cannot exist without the dark
and the light; neither can you.

Reflection 83
Wisdom
When you don't know the answers to
something, just admit it. You're only human,
and there's nothing wrong with occasionally
being wrong.

Reflection 84
Wisdom
The smooth and cracked parts of you symbolize the significant parts of being all of you. Embrace it. Embody it. Accept it, and you'll never regret it.

Reflection 85
Enlightenment
I don't just deal with my life; I feel and heal through my life, embodying self-love for myself because I have a hearty desire to spiritually grow and evolve.

Reflection 86
Motivation
The power is within you. Allow it to pivot right through you to become an upgraded version of you.

Reflection 87
Food for Thought
Eternal question for life: Who am I?
As one changes, the answers to this same
question change.

Reflection 88
Grounding Practice
Be present, pause, and allow these magical
moments to shift your thoughts and emotions
to pass through the soles of your feet down
through the core roots of the earth. This is the
perfect way to consolidate your energy, find
balance, and re-connect to our dear Mother
Earth.

Reflection 89
Inspiration
Sometimes the blessings magically appear when you're not trying and you're just being.

Reflection 90
Wisdom
Be like the owl that astutely observes from a starlit point of view while turning its head and soaring through the dark and light times of life.

Reflection 91
Wisdom
Whether in the battlefield as a Warrior or on the bench in reset mode, a true Warrior will always remain a Warrior because they have the wisdom to know when to tackle life head-on and when to sit, rest, redefine, and align.

Reflection 92
Authenticity
Your authentic self follows you around like your shadow. Stop running away from it, and be it.

Reflection 93
Trust and Faith
Take chances in life regardless of the circumstances. No risk, no reward.

Reflection 94
Wisdom
Light and unconditional love are available at all times. All you have to do is connect to your physical heart and breathe in love while exhaling love out into the world.

Reflection 95
Wisdom
How many times do you have to touch a hot stove to know it's hot? Every burn is different but it still stings.

Reflection 96
Finding Peace
Find joy and fulfillment from within and you'll never be or feel alone.

Reflection 97
Spiritual Awakening
Without uncomfortable change, there is no room for personal growth and self-revelation.

Reflection 98
Authenticity
If you have to fake it or lie, thinking you're being your authentic self, think again. You are enough just as you are.

Reflection 99
Wisdom
The teacher usually knows the answer. That doesn't mean they gloat about knowing the answer. A good teacher leads the student to find the answer with immense care and concern. Humility is a virtue.

Reflection 100
Wisdom
You're never neglected because you're always protected and supported by the universe.

Reflection 101
Motivation
Success is accepting that whether one wins or loses, one keeps on trying.

Reflection 102
Inner Strength
You cannot get stronger without resistance. By challenging yourself, you build momentum and great stamina from within.

Reflection 103

Wisdom

The heart and soul represent the truth of who you are, unconditional love that feels and heals through everything.

Reflection 104

Wisdom

People will attempt to steal, manipulate, and betray you, but the two things that cannot be taken from you are your dignity and self-respect.

Reflection 105

Wisdom

If you have a limited perception of life in a box, don't expect a vantage point of view.

Reflection 106
Finding Courage
Stand in your power even when you're shaking in your boots.

Reflection 107
Wisdom
You never really overcome the stages of grief and trauma. Rather, you get through it.

Reflection 108
Wisdom
When you value yourself, you find value in everything and with everyone.

Reflection 109
Kindness and Compassion Practice
Pay it forward by doing kind things for a stranger.

Name three tasks and/or gestures that are achievable to help out your fellow brother or sister.

Reflection 110
Wisdom
When making a decision, look both ways just as when you cross the street. Only then can you be proactive and make wiser choices with clarity versus regret.

Reflection 111
Wisdom
A diamond cannot shine its brilliance without sitting in the dark of the coal mines.

Reflection 112
Authenticity
People will judge you left and right; let them. As long as you aren't hurting anybody including yourself, march forward in life knowing and being your zesty self.

Reflection 113
Positive Affirmation
Nobody stops me from being me, except me. I am unstoppable.

Reflection 114
Wisdom
Human beings are like trees. Some are short, some are tall. Some are fat, and some are skinny. But that's what makes the world so enriched with beauty.

Reflection 115
Wisdom
Let others play their own sport their own way on their own time. Meanwhile, enjoy playing your own sport on your turf; it's much more fun and compelling that way.

Reflection 116
Wisdom
Be the champion of your own game whether you win or lose. Do your best; that's a true testament of real success.

Reflection 117
Wisdom
Your burns and bruises are experiences that
shape-shifted you into the person you are
today. Be grateful not resentful.

Reflection 118
Compassion
There's really only one ingredient to show
somebody compassion: a heart.
Any human that is "being" is capable of this.

Reflection 119
Amla's Insight
People prey on my dignity like bumble bees on
pollen. But like the blossom, I revive, radiating
my pure essence.

Reflection 120
Mehta Mantra
I accept my flaws.
I am full of finesse.
I am fabulous.
So it is.
(Repeat)

Reflection 121
Intuition
I see from my heart, and, at the same time, I
feel and sense my body telling me exactly what
it needs when it needs it.

Reflection 122
Being Whole
Listen to the heartfelt answers from within.
Keep them nestled within the nub of your soul
and continue being whole.

Reflection 123
Wisdom
Power stems from your gut. Passion stems from your heart. Don't mix up the two. Both are needed to live an abundant and optimal life.

Reflection 124
Speaking Your Truth
I cannot help you if you refuse to be helped. Just ask.

Reflection 125
Standing in Your Power
Compromise. But do not compromise yourself, including your moral standards and ethics, for anybody else.

Reflection 126
Motivation
You are meant to propel through life in low, medium, and high velocities. Keep on moving and ascending through the majestic skies of your personal journey.

Reflection 127
Wisdom
Your desire to be empowered requires experiencing disempowerment. Your desire to experience unconditional love requires experiencing a broken heart. Your desire to be respected requires being disrespected. That goes to show you that when there is no pain there is no gain.

Reflection 128

An Awakening

Sometimes the pain is so embedded within the nooks and crannies of your body, mind, and spirit, it must erupt like an earthquake to shake up your entire being so that you can jumpstart the process of hope and healing.

Reflection 129

Sensory Practice

Using all five senses, I challenge you to take 15 to 30 minutes to share:

What do you see?

What do you smell?

What do you hear?

What do you sense/taste?

What textures can you touch?

By tapping into all five senses, you can fully experience the present.

Reflection 130
Wisdom
You can prepare all you want for a forecasted blizzard with shovels, sand, and salt. But until the storm has come and gone, only time will tell when to resume back to normality and clean up. This is the story of life.

Reflection 131
Wisdom
When you are honoring yourself, there is no need to explain yourself; it's a feeling of freedom and liberation.

Reflection 132
Steps to Enlightenment
Sometimes experiencing the pain and suffering is the only way to awaken and walk through the dark tunnel to align yourself one step at a time towards the light.

Reflection 133
Amla's Insight
The same experiences I initially thought restricted and tied me down enabled me to ignite my "Amla Power" inside-out.

Reflection 134
Wisdom
Just because you're in the kitchen doesn't mean you're the chef. Don't assume that wherever you are, you must take on the role of a leader. You're not meant to be an expert in everything you do. You're meant to learn from everything you do.

Reflection 135
Unconditional Love
Pour your own cup of love and let it overflow into the universe.

Reflection 136
Wisdom
First and foremost, only expect the best from yourself. This way you'll never be let down and/or disappointed by anyone else.

Reflection 137
Mehta Mantra
I am here.
I am healthy.
I am happy.
So it is.
(Repeat)

Reflection 138
Compassion Exercise
Name three simple, yet effective, ways you feel you can make a difference in this world, and then follow through.

Reflection 139
Acceptance
One must accept the milk has spilled to clean it up one drop at a time.

Reflection 140
Wisdom
The deeper and steeper the heartbreak, the more one has the capacity to feel in order to heal throughout life.

Reflection 141
Wisdom
Efficient and effective communication is generated by having open and honest conversations no matter how difficult the circumstances may be.

Reflection 142
Mehta Mantra
I am a brilliant being of light and love.
So it is.
(Repeat)

Reflection 143
Wisdom
Surround yourself with faces, spaces, and places where you are celebrated and not crushed. In the end, you're in charge of who to invite into your life.

Reflection 144
Motivation
You can accomplish anything in life because you commit and refuse to quit.

Reflection 145
Love
Being in love is like sautéing vegetables on a hot stove; the food/love needs to marinate in order for the savory flavors to permeate through the room.

Reflection 146
Authenticity
It takes just as much time and effort to conform with others as it does to be your authentic self. You decide how you want to spend your time.

Reflection 147
Amla's Insight
I was down on my hands and knees begging the universe, please, please, give me the inner strength to rise above and get up again. It didn't happen overnight; it took incredible willpower to gradually step up onto a higher platform for my holiest good. It goes to show, nothing happens to you; it happens for you on the path of evolution.

Reflection 148
Authenticity
Being your authentic self means staying grounded with your core values and belief system no matter how many times the weather pattern changes.

Reflection 149
Self-Care
More times than not you must recharge your mind, body, and spirit in order to take charge and accelerate through your life.

Reflection 150
Unconditional Love
Real love is like air; it's felt, not seen, and it's always available for everyone.

Reflection 151
Amla's Insight
What if I seriously questioned whether or not I should hop in the car and drive even though I have partial vision. Not only would I endanger myself but also others driving on the road. Being a part of humankind is taking responsibility for yourself while being altruistic to all of mankind.

Reflection 152
Intuition
Your first choice is usually the right choice. Trust yourself; you've got this.

Reflection 153
Wisdom
A healthy relationship is like waiting for a gourmet meal. Enjoy the finest, it's worth your valuable time.

Reflection 154
Mehta Mantra
I have faith in myself.
I am free and liberated.
I am complete.
So it is.
(Repeat)

Reflection 155
Wisdom
Be like the ripples of water within a river that flows over and around the boulders, sticks, stones, and even people. Nature always finds its way over and through the obstacles and so can you.

Reflection 156
Wisdom
Just because the odometer reaches 100 mph
doesn't mean you drive that speed. Freedom is
a privilege; proceed with caution.

Reflection 157
Wisdom
Being on the journey of life is like running a
marathon. It's your race and you can crawl,
walk, or run at your own pace to reach the
finish line in divine time.

Reflection 158
Trust and Faith
Hope and faith keeps my spirit up high
through the interchangeable tides of life.

Reflection 159
Inspiration
Whether the mountain is a hill or Mount Everest, it's your own mountain to climb. Go for it and get climbing.

Reflection 160
Wisdom
People are like revolving doors, coming in and out of your life. The key is to enjoy the allotted time you have when the "guest" arrives.

Detach when it's time for them to leave. And because nothing is permanent, there's always another person lingering around to enter your front door.

Reflection 161
Authenticity
When you define yourself by what you do,
there are no guarantees. When you live by
being you, there's always a guarantee of
reflecting the best within you.

Reflection 162
Amla's Insight
People always ask me, "Amla, how do you see?"
I reverse the question and ask, "Well, how do
you see?" Everyone has their own perceptions
of life, and so it is.

Reflection 163
Wisdom
With the set intention of love and compassion,
you have every right to do what feels right for
you.

Reflection 164
Connecting With Your Inner Child
Tap into that energetic inner child and do three simple things to transform an autopilot day into a playful and fun-loving day. It could be anything that makes your heart zing.
1. You could grab some colored pencils and draw.
2. Build with playing cards.
3. Go outside and collect some rocks and paint them.

It's the simple things in life that lighten and brighten you.

Reflection 165
Wisdom
A closed mind cannot open new and limitless possibilities.

Reflection 166
Amla's Insight
If I shine too brightly for you, wear sunglasses.
I will shine anyway.

Reflection 167
Wisdom
If you reach a fork in the road, you can choose
resistance or resilience. But whatever you
choose, there's always an opportunity to learn
a life lesson.

Reflection 168
Wisdom
Do people actually listen to try to understand
you, or do they just hear you and move right
along? Know the difference and use
discernment.

Reflection 169
Amla's Revelation
I don't need you to save me; I need you to have faith and trust in me.

Reflection 170
Joy
Happiness doesn't require being positive all day long. Happiness and joy stem from accepting the present moment for what it is, "as is."

Reflection 171
Inspiration
Be like Superman or Wonder Woman; without the "bad guys" and experiences, they couldn't use their superpowers.

Reflection 172
Mehta Mantra
Four Mehta mantras to uplift you each and
every day:
I believe.
I trust.
I love.
I accept.
So it is.
(Repeat)

Reflection 173
Self-Empowerment
Sometimes taking back your life means taking
back your power.

Reflection 174
Intuition
Use your inner-knowingness like a road map traveling along the path of life. You'll never be lost.

Reflection 175
Wisdom
Start your day like a jet airplane taking off for its final destination. You wake up fresh, "fueled," and ready to go. During the mid-day hours you stay steady in plateau mode. And in the evening, you may wind down by taking time for your family while nurturing yourself so that you can land your day safely with peace and tranquility.

Reflection 176
Setting Healthy Boundaries
Your "boundary button" will be pushed and
probed until you say "no."

Reflection 177
Self-Awareness
Awareness is not about physically seeing;
awareness requires three main ingredients:
   1. Tap into your own frequency.
   2. Focus on your intention and attention.
   3. Feel, sense, and embody
      consciousness.

Reflection 178
Wisdom
When people tell you what you should be
feeling, walk away. Trust yourself; your feelings
represent the trail markers en route to
self-care.

Reflection 179
Wisdom
The only thing that is consistent in life is the notion of inconsistency.

Reflection 180
Being Grounded
Be grounded and robust like an oak tree. While your thoughts and emotions sway back and forth like branches during a storm, the roots of you never change.

Reflection 181
Wisdom
It doesn't matter why people alter themselves with their bottomless ego and pride; it's their basic way to hide.

Reflection 182
Acceptance
If you cannot keep up with me, I accept this and set you free.

Reflection 183
Mehta Mantra
I am fearless.
I am courageous.
I am relentless.
So it is.
(Repeat)

Reflection 184
Unconditional Love
I see your authentic face tucked within my heart space.

Reflection 185
Positive Affirmation
Everywhere I am, I am awake and aware.

Reflection 186
Unconditional Love
Slow dance to the harmonious melodies of your sacred heart and soul.

Reflection 187
Amla's Revelation
I'm standing in my power, dancing to the rhythm of my stride. I'm standing in my power, as a warrior woman with nothing to hide.

Reflection 188
Wisdom
You cannot detach from something if you're not attached to something in the first place.

Reflection 189
Food for Thought
What if being strong is letting go, and letting go is being strong?

Reflection 190
Authenticity
A baby will laugh at a funeral and cry at a wedding. Being authentic is anywhere and everywhere you are.

Reflection 191
Trust and Faith
Universe, you got me into the whirlwind vortex; I have faith and trust you will get me out.

Reflection 192
Self-Care
Nobody knows when you're thirsty. You are the only one who can quench your own thirst.

Reflection 193
Faith and Trust
When I find it difficult to receive help even when I ask, I remember not to look laterally, but to look straight up to the universe because I acknowledge I am solely and soulfully supported.

Reflection 194
Love and Nurture
What would you tell your inner child who's
scared of the "monster" underneath their bed?
How would you lovingly comfort your inner
child who just wants the "monster" to
disappear?

Transmute the fear from within by filling
yourself up with unconditional love. Love
prevails over fear.

Reflection 195
Mehta Mantra
Be quiet.
Be still.
Be ready to feel.
This is the perfect recipe to fully heal.
(Repeat)

Reflection 196
Amla's Insight
When I physically cannot see, I would have seen it all.

Reflection 197
Happiness
Sometimes you find the most rewarding treasures when you enjoy the simple pleasures in your life.

Reflection 198
Trust and Faith
Having faith means having no expectations of the outcome and believing everything happens for your highest potential. How do you maintain faith in yourself?

Reflection 199
Self-Love
You have nothing to lose when you devote your time to spoon-feeding your heart with delicious love.

Reflection 200
Wisdom
When you are simply being, knowing that everything is impermanent, including your own life, it adds profound meaning to the existence of life.

Reflection 201
Amla's Insight
The truth is untainted, opaque, and electrifying. I will always speak my truth.

Reflection 202
Wisdom
Your frequency attracts mirror-like energy.

Reflection 203
Wisdom
Without digging out the sticks, stones, and shrubs within your spiritual garden of life, you cannot plant new seeds.

Reflection 204
A Fresh Start
You cannot go on your dream vacation using an old stuffed suitcase. You must unpack the old to live it up and do something exciting and new.

Reflection 205
Kindness and Compassion
Be compassionate with all beings "just because." It gives exponential meaning to the art of giving from your heart.

Reflection 206
Food for Thought
You can live your life like you're a caged animal and still find freedom from within, or live a privileged lifestyle and feel like you're living like a wild animal in the jungle. What narrative do you choose to live?

Reflection 207
Care and Compassion
I don't hear you. I do my best to be present and conscientiously listen to you.

Reflection 208
Setting Healthy Boundaries
Don't tell me I can't because I will and I can!

Reflection 209
Enlightenment
Being in the darkness isn't the scary part. It's facing the inevitable underlying misconceptions and perceptions of the truth of who you are - unconditional love.

Reflection 210
Speaking Your Truth
I see through the subtle layers of lies, so stop wearing a disguise.

Reflection 211
Wisdom
You can always trust your heartline, but not necessarily your bloodline.

Reflection 212
Setting Healthy Boundaries
Don't tell me how I should feel. My feelings are just that, mine.

Reflection 213
Mehta Mantra
I hold onto nothing to receive everything.
So it is.
(Repeat)

Reflection 214
Wisdom
If you're always playing it safe, it's like parking the car in neutral. You're in the same spot not growing, and not going anywhere.

Reflection 215
Food for Thought
It takes just as much work and effort to be competitive as it does to be your original self.

Write down when you feel the need to push yourself to excel or fire up that passion. How do you find balance using your heartspace versus your headspace?

Reflection 216
Bliss
I am not happy just because the sun is shining.
I am happy because I am shining from within.

Reflection 217
Mehta Mantra
The truth in me honors the truth in you.

Reflection 218
Wisdom
Just call the problem what it is versus what it's not. After all, you cannot reach for a Band-Aid in the medicine cabinet to heal and/or recover from a "broken leg" wound.

Reflection 219
The Art of Success
There are three main ingredients to being successful.
1. Being patient.
2. Being persistent.
3. Being committed towards your goal.

Reflection 220
Enlightenment
You have to experience the extreme polarities of life to maintain an equanimous life.

Reflection 221
Wisdom
Knowledge is power. Don't abuse it; just use it
for your highest good.

Reflection 222
Authenticity
When you walk your own strut, it gives you a
sense of self-confidence. Work it with great
pizzazz.

Reflection 223
Self-Care Ho'oponopono Prayer
A wonderful way to start and end the day is to recite the Hawaiian prayer with an intention for yourself and for the world. (Traditionally there are four affirmations; I added my own two favorites.)

Original:
    I love you.
    I forgive you.
    I am grateful.
    I am sorry.
My added favorites:
    I respect you.
    I accept you.
    (Repeat)

Reflection 224
Wisdom
Listening to others is a self-mastery art and skill.

Reflection 225
Gratitude Practice
I'm grateful that my heart is beating, that I still can see, and that I am blessed. Name three things you are grateful for.

Reflection 226
Setting Healthy Boundaries
Like a building with its concrete foundation, maintaining healthy boundaries gives you the feeling of safety and security for optimum health and wellness.

Reflection 227
Spiritual Practice
In order to connect to your heart space, repeat the sacred sound of creation from the ancient language of India, Sanskrit, "Om." Pronounced "Ohm," it works wonders to feel and sense peace from within.

Reflection 228
Wisdom
When you are "soul-self-serving," you know you are full of unconditional love.

Reflection 229
Wisdom
Think of your feelings as batteries in a remote control. You need the positive and negative charges to live an enlightened life.

Reflection 230
Food for Thought
You are innately created to open and contract.
If the heart does that internally, why wouldn't
you do that externally?

Reflection 231
Mehta Mantra
I am home when I connect with spirit.

Reflection 232
Positive Affirmation
I warmly welcome people into my life because
they accept me into their life just as I am.

Reflection 233
Amla's Insight
Somebody once told me I should be used to ignorance. Ironically enough, this person was the ignorant one. I will never grow accustomed to ignorance because in any way, shape, or form, choosing ignorance is not acceptable.

Reflection 234
Wisdom
Forgiveness without whole-heart intention is meaningless.

Reflection 235
Wisdom
Sometimes people appear to want to help you with good intentions but end up inadvertently hindering you because they are actually doing what's best for them, not for you. Always do what feels right for you, straight from the heart.

Reflection 236
Food for Thought
Why do we, as humans, question when we are sad or unhappy? When we are happy, we usually accept the feeling with open arms. Throughout the process of self-realization, one must accept the "positive" and "negative" thoughts, emotions, and feelings equally to maintain equanimity.

Reflection 237
Food for Thought
Do you conform with the crowd because it's the right thing to do? Or, does it feel right for you? You decide.

Reflection 238
"I Am" Meditation
1. Silently whisper "I am" while taking in a deep breath.
2. Pause.
3. Exhale.
4. Repeat.

Reflection 239
Setting Healthy Boundaries
Establishing healthy boundaries is like being a teacher. You must repeat the boundary or lesson several times before the "student" learns.

Reflection 240
Self-Care Practice
Taking time to ground, recenter, and renew
yourself during the day is extremely
important.

What do you do to reboot and balance
yourself? Journal for five minutes. Hug a tree.
Listen to soothing music. Make it "do-able" for
you.

Reflection 241
Positive Affirmation
I recharge and connect with myself especially
when I feel disconnected.

Reflection 242
Food for Thought
Imagine if your doctor diagnosed you with COVID-19 and bluntly said, "you're not the only one going through this." How would you feel? Until you personally experience your own uphill battles in life, nobody has any right to dismiss or make any judgments upon anyone else.

Reflection 243
Acceptance
Adapt and change according to what the universe reveals to you, not to what others do or tell you.

Reflection 244
Positive Affirmation
I am open to receive infinite miracles and blessings throughout the day.

Reflection 245
Self-Empowerment
Treat yourself like a rockstar on stage whether or not the spotlight is on or off of you.

Reflection 246
Authenticity
If you keep on rejecting me, that's okay. I take it as my queue to keep on sparkling anyway.

Reflection 247
Amla's Insight
Society might label me as disabled. However, I consider myself distinctively "abled."

Reflection 248
Personal Growth
The gifts of stillness, silence, and meditation have taught me to find deep meaning and depth in my life. What has helped you to expand and grow?

Reflection 249
Wisdom
Find liberation in yourself by unconditionally loving yourself.

Reflection 250
Personal Growth
Name something tangible you'd like to learn today. Life is short, do it.

Reflection 251
Authenticity
Come back to me if and when you are ready to
accept all of me.

Reflection 252
Manifestation
Within the manifestation process it's essential
to believe in limitless possibilities. What steps
do you take in order to accomplish your
particular goals? Be patient with yourself. If it's
that important to you, you'll continue to take
the necessary steps to transform your deepest
wants and desires into reality.

Reflection 253
Setting Healthy Boundaries
If you tell me I have one minute of your time, I deserve the full 60 seconds of your attention.

Reflection 254
Spiritual Practice
"Om So Hum" is an ancient Sanksrit mantra which means, "I am the sound of the universe." Repeat this mantra to connect with God, Source, Creator, and yourself.

Reflection 255
Amla's Insight
My third eye symbolizes my superpower; my "real teacher" leading me in endless possibilities that I never could've envisioned for myself.

Reflection 256
Wisdom
Don't be like the side dish in life. Be and treat yourself like you're the main entrée. You are worthy and deserving of being the center of attention.

Reflection 257
Being Present
Sometimes you need to revisit your past to understand your present. Notice if you are reliving it or just visiting it. There's a big difference.

Reflection 258
Wisdom
Stroll on the long stretch beach of life leaving behind your legendary footprints in the sand.

Reflection 259
Personal Growth
I moved on and away from you because I realized I fell in love with the layers of lies you chose to wrap around you, rather than you, being you.

Reflection 260
Inspiration
Don't be afraid to give your everything to achieve anything. You give it your best shot and that's worth a lot.

Reflection 261
Wisdom
People will attempt to block you and stop you from moving up the spiral staircase of enlightenment. That's okay; it's your own flight of stairs to climb. Move at your own pace, one step at time.

Reflection 262
Wisdom
You don't need any validation to take care of yourself. Nobody can take care of you better than you.

Reflection 263
Wisdom
You are not born knowing everything and you don't die knowing everything. Stop living like you know everything, be humbled, and understand that your life is a novelty, a gift. Enjoy!

Reflection 264
Gratitude Practice
Thank you.
(Pause)
Thank you.
(Pause)
Thank you,
universe.
(Pause)
Love,
<your name>
(Repeat)

Reflection 265
Wisdom
Don't get overwhelmed with the number of storms you have been through. Think of them as unexpected opportunities to excel and be a lively, new you.

Reflection 266
Mehta Mantra
Be Love.
Do it with Love.
(Repeat)

Reflection 267
Self-Care Practice
Name three intangible qualities that you value
about yourself. How do these particular values
serve your life purpose?

Reflection 268
Food for Thought
Sometimes it's not a matter of
overthinking and asking why. It's a matter of
asking, 'what do I have to lose?'

Reflection 269
Unconditional Love
By bathing in the beauty of love and light, your soul purpose is always right.

Reflection 270
Love
You won't grab my attention by showing me affection. You'll grab my attention by your loving vibration.

Reflection 271
Speaking Your Truth
You don't own me; therefore, you have no right to control me.

Reflection 272
Perseverance
When we fall, we fall; it's our choice to build a
wall or to bounce back again.

Reflection 273
Speaking Your Truth
I will let go when I am ready and able, not
because that's what you think I should do.

Reflection 274
Wisdom
You don't all of a sudden turn the age of 75.
You grow, adapt, and change to each and every
age you experience.

Reflection 275
Food for Thought Exercise
If you could only live with three tangible things for the rest of your life, what would they be and why?

Reflection 276
Unconditional Love Practice
I miss the days when we could spontaneously hug one another. Although if I really need that tender love and care, I cross my right arm over my left shoulder and my left arm over my right shoulder to give myself a gentle squeeze. Show yourself self-love; you are lovable.

Reflection 277
Wisdom
Imagine a high school student walking up to a second grader and telling them what they are reading is super easy, and wait until they read Shakespeare. Meanwhile, the second grader is freaking out trying to read, "A mouse ran out of the house." No matter what stage of life you're in, it's not harder or easier than another person's; it's just different.

Reflection 278
Authenticity
We all wear stitches. Some are visible and some are not; wear them with pride.

Reflection 279
Setting Healthy Boundaries
If I occasionally need space and time away
from you, it's because I care, and I am
mindfully trying to be a better person for
myself and you.

Reflection 280
Wisdom
A deep person cannot get along with a shallow
person and vice versa. It may be nice for a
while but just like wading in the kiddie
swimming pool, eventually the person will get
bored and outgrow the shallow end and
challenge themselves by plunging into the
deep end.

Reflection 281
Setting Healthy Boundaries
I don't ask for much but when I do, please listen and follow through.

Reflection 282
Self-Empowerment
Stop living like a prisoner serving a life sentence and break free from the shackled limitations and belief systems.

Reflection 283
Enlightenment
Transmute your pain and suffering into sacred nuggets of life lessons, guiding you along the path of nirvana.

Reflection 284
Self-Care Practice
Do everything with honor and grace.
Name three ways you honor yourself.

Reflection 285
Speaking Your Truth
I don't care what you think of me, I care about
what I think of me.

Reflection 286
Wisdom
People are like stars in the galaxy; each one
twinkles differently yet they all exist within the
same cosmos.

Reflection 287
Wisdom
The expert was once a beginner who succeeds by staying focused on the goal one experience at a time.

Reflection 288
Amla's Insight
I have been treated like a princess, with people offering to help me throughout my day. And I have been treated like garbage due to ignorance. How others treat me is a reflection of themselves, not me. Nevertheless, I will always treat myself like a queen of unconditional love.

Reflection 289
Acceptance Exercise
Reflect upon a time where you experienced full acceptance; no judgment.

How did this particular experience make you feel? Were you at peace with yourself? If so, please feel free to explain.

Reflection 290
Wisdom
Giving and receiving is like taking one full breath (inhale and exhale). You need both to survive and sustain equilibrium.

Reflection 291
Mehta Mantra
I am accountable and responsible for my words and actions. So it is.

Reflection 292
Wisdom
Let go of the worry and shame to eliminate self-blame.

Reflection 293
Root Chakra
There are seven main energy centers (also known as chakras) within the body. By stating the affirmations tethered to each energy center, along with imagining each color associated with each chakra, one is able to revitalize and find balance within the mind, body, and spirit. Reflections 293 through 299 are an energy body cleanse.

The first energy center is called the "root chakra."
Color: Red
Located at the base of the spine.

Root chakra affirmation:
I am safe.
I am anchored.
I am home.
So it is.

Reflection 294
Second Chakra
The second energy center is called the "sacral chakra."
Color: Orange
The sacral chakra is located below the belly button.

Sacral chakra affirmation:
I am a manifester.
I am creative.
I experience pleasure and joy.
So it is.

Reflection 295
Third Chakra
The third energy center is the "solar plexus chakra."
Color: Sunshine yellow
The solar plexus chakra is the area just above the navel, extending across the lower ribs.

Solar plexus affirmation:
I am confident.
I am empowered.
I am motivated to pursue my sole purpose.
So it is.

Reflection 296
Fourth Chakra
The fourth energy center is the "heart chakra."
Color: Green
The heart chakra is located at the heart center.

Heart chakra affirmation:
I am lovable.
I am compassionate.
I give and receive straight from the heart.
So it is.

Reflection 297
Fifth Chakra
The fifth energy center is called the "throat chakra."
Color: Blue
The throat chakra is located at the throat.

Throat chakra affirmation:
I openly speak my truth.
I am self-expressive.
I communicate efficiently and effectively with myself and others.
So it is.

Reflection 298
Sixth Chakra
The sixth energy center is the "third eye chakra."
Color: Indigo
The Third Eye is located in the center of your forehead in between your eyebrows.

Third Eye chakra affirmation:
I am a visionary.
I am intuitive and insightful.
I am full of wisdom.
So it is.

Reflection 299
Seventh Chakra
The seventh energy center is the "crown chakra."
Color: Violet
The Crown chakra is located on top of your head.

Crown chakra affirmation:
I am always supported and connected to Source and Creator.
I am an infinite spark of light and love.
I am a unique soul.

Congratulations! You have finished a full-body chakra cleanse!

Reflection 300
Wisdom
With a closed fist it's harder to receive your heart's desires. With a hand wide open it's harder to take hold and receive your truest desires. Giving is as equally important as it is to receive.

Reflection 301
Wisdom
You can encounter a positive person and have a negative experience or vice-versa. You can have a positive experience with a somewhat negative person. You'll never feel off kilter when you accept people are just people trying to have a human experience.

Reflection 302
Amla's Insight
When you close your eyes, you cannot see. There are no excuses for not understanding blindness.

Reflection 303
Wisdom
The older I get, the less I regret because all of the intricate pieces of me are magnified and exposed for myself, the Creator, and for all eyes that choose to see me.

Reflection 304
Wisdom
Sometimes it all makes sense inside of you when nothing makes sense outside of you.

Reflection 305
Mehta Mantra
I am self-full by being kind and compassionate with myself and of service to others.
(Repeat)

Reflection 306
Wisdom
Honesty is the soul food for an effervescent livelihood.

Reflection 307
Mehta Mantra
I am whole being my true self.
So it is.
(Repeat)

Reflection 308
Amla's Insight
I physically see like I am swimming through skim milk. At the same time, I have never felt so full from within.

Reflection 309
Enlightenment
When I feel happy, healed, and complete, it's like hiking up a treacherous mountain peak and being present while enjoying a breathtaking view, symbolizing a spiritual gift from the universe made just for me.

Reflection 310
Wisdom
Phony people like frou frou answers. Meanwhile, the trustworthy person is habitually on a quest for the truth within the answers.

Reflection 311
Being Whole
When you feel whole and anchored down to
the soles of your feet, nobody can make you
feel less than or depleted.

Reflection 312
Wisdom
Notice when people try to belittle you. At the
end of the day, they are the ones that feel little
about themselves.

Reflection 313
Trust and Faith
Every challenge I have been through,
spiritually, mentally, emotionally, and
physically has been a test of faith and trust.
There are perks to facing hardships.

Reflection 314
Setting Healthy Boundaries
Let me be me, while I let you be you.

Reflection 315
Mehta Mantra
I am love.
So it is.
(Repeat)

Reflection 316
Self-Love Practice
Being present can be as basic as placing your hand on your heart and feeling your heartbeat pulsing through your entire being. A gentle reminder that you are fresh and alive.

Reflection 317
Inspiration
Great leaders lift their team up when they are down and don't push their team down when they are rising up.

Reflection 318
Food for Thought
Nowadays if you call out bad behavior you often become the scapegoat. When did doing the right thing become labeled as a "bad thing?" Just do the right thing; you'll sleep better at night.

Reflection 319
Positive Affirmation
I am never alone because I treat myself like a rare gemstone.

Reflection 320
Gratitude
If you're going to pick a "tude," choose the attitude of gratitude, and wake up every morning and say thank you to the universe.

Reflection 321
Self-Care Practice
Meditation is a meaningful practice to ground and stay centered. This doesn't mean to sit in silence in the cross-legged lotus position for endless hours. Think of meditation as a time to pause, quiet the mind, and get still whether it be observing your breath or being out in nature.

If you practice this for five minutes a day, it soothes and softens your mind, body, and spirit. Namaste. Meaning: The light in me honors the light in you.

Reflection 322
Self-Respect
Always express and deliver your message with truth and triumph.

Reflection 323
Speaking Your Truth
I cannot be my authentic self if I am not my raw and real self.

Reflection 324
Wisdom
Remember that one cannot always receive exactly what they want. Although the universe always provides for what one needs.

Reflection 325
Wisdom
Don't let your ego dictate and drive your human "beingness." Instead, let your ego "go" for the ride in the trunk of your car and use it sparingly.

Reflection 326
Authenticity
Your so-called flaws are where the sweet cells of unconditional love co-exist with one another.

Reflection 327
Forgiveness
Saying sorry too soon can be detrimental rather than beneficial. Only apologize when you actually mean it.

Reflection 328
Trust and Faith
I cannot imagine a life without hope and faith
whisking me towards my signature destiny.

Reflection 329
Authenticity
I am a masterpiece of original art whether I am
seen or not.

Reflection 330
Self-Empowerment
If you stop trying, most likely you won't
achieve anything. As long as your heart keeps
pumping, keep on going.

Reflection 331
Speaking Your Truth
If you want to help me then say, "Yes." If you don't want to help me, tell me the truth and say, "No." Just be honest.

Reflection 332
Mehta Mantra
I am the master of my life.
I am purposeful.
I am peaceful.
So it is.
(Repeat)

Reflection 333
Setting Healthy Boundaries
Always walk into a space or place knowing
some people will say "Yes" to you while others
will say "No" to you. Invite the yes-people with
open arms and tactfully close the door on the
no-people.

Reflection 334
Wisdom
I know that I am never alone because
unconditional love never abandons me.

Reflection 335
Positive Affirmation
Because I am a kind-hearted person, I
appreciate each and every person.

Reflection 336

Wisdom

You cannot poke and prod people to see something. It's like telling a blind person to physically see and identify something. The individual is simply not able to see. Acceptance is a virtue.

Reflection 337

Wisdom

Solitude does not mean you're lonely. It's a purposeful time to realign with the divine and connect with your sovereign self.

Reflection 338
Acceptance
Accepting people as they are is like being grateful for Aunt Sally's strawberry rhubarb pie at the Thanksgiving dinner table. You don't really like that flavor of pie but you love and adore Aunt Sally and you accept what she brought to the table with love, admiration, and respect for her.

Reflection 339
Amla's Revelation
I am going blind, not brainless. Please don't underestimate me, and respect me, for me.

Reflection 340
Wisdom
Be like a firecracker, shooting straight up through the midnight sky, bursting with vibrant colors of light for all to see.

Reflection 341
Manifestation
You'll never manifest exactly what you want unless you set forth an intention and aim for exactly what you want. Be like the person who only craves chocolate ice cream no matter how many flavors are offered to you. Don't settle for less than what you desire. Even if it's as simple as getting your favorite flavor of ice cream.

Reflection 342
Wisdom
It's perfectly fine to rest and restore when you feel exhausted or are at your wit's end in life. Without routine rest and sleep, we, as human beings, wouldn't be able to survive and thrive throughout our daily lives.

Reflection 343
Hope and Healing
Every time I've healed from a broken heart, I was never the same again – each time being replenished and reborn all over again.

Reflection 344
Food for Thought
Why would you chase people who are running away from you? The more you're chasing, the more the other person is running. I finally stopped doing this when I found the most freakishly amazing, reliable, and remarkable person in my life: me!

Reflection 345
Happiness
If you are loyal to me, you are golden to me.

Reflection 346
Brain Balance Practice
The infinity symbol (sideways eight) symbolizes endless possibilities.
Imagine and trace the infinity symbol from your left side of the brain hemisphere to your right side of the brain hemisphere. This helps you to be centered and focused while finding inner-peace.

Practice this as many times as you wish. It's a fabulous way to reduce stress and anxiety.

Reflection 347
Authenticity
I am like the sun. I don't dim my light to be accepted by others. I shine on everything and with everyone.

Reflection 348
Food for Thought
Passive aggressive people love being around
straight forward people because they
acknowledge exactly where they stand with
the other person. Meanwhile, the straight
forward person spends numerous hours trying
to understand the last five-minute encounter
with the passive aggressive person.

Reflection 349
Acceptance
If you fall in love with my no-nonsense
frequency, my scars, and my individuality,
that's showing me you truly accept me.

Reflection 350
Pure Love Affirmation
I feel deeply to love deeply.

Reflection 351
Speaking Your Truth
I will always ask if I need something. With that, if I really needed your opinion, I'd ask for it.

Reflection 352
Wisdom
I won myself over because I am one with myself and the universe.

Reflection 353
Optimism
Think of the present as a chance to reinvent yourself into a beautiful new you!

Reflection 354
Wisdom
Think of your soul like a satellite dish revolving
around the planet Earth that represents your
body, mind, and spirit. There is no judgment
because your soul identifies with your body "as
just a body" – a gentle reminder that you are a
soul-being first, and, secondly, a human that is
"just being."

Reflection 355
Wisdom
As human beings, we subconsciously
undermine the soul's way of being everything
and nothing simultaneously.

Reflection 356
Mehta Mantra
I am balanced.
I am heart-centered.
The universe enables me to discover how I can serve myself and serve humanity at the same time.
(Repeat.)

Reflection 357
Enlightenment
When your heart bleeds the pain and suffering, don't let it consume you; allow it to penetrate through you in order to heal the infinite layers of you.

Reflection 358
Wisdom
There are three main ingredients to
accomplish anything in your life:
1. Being consistent
2. Being diligent
3. Trying again after failure

Remember this when you are on the verge of
throwing your hands up and quitting.

Reflection 359
Ascension Process
Every moment you have the opportunity to
rise higher than the moment before, do it.

Reflection 360
Wisdom
When something triggers you, it's okay to take things personally. Without it, there's no room for personal growth.

Reflection 361
Self-Care
Love and nurture yourself like you would take care of your favorite houseplant.

Reflection 362
Amla's Insight
I feel like I'm Dorothy in a scene from the movie, "The Wizard of Oz." When I had clearer physical vision, I felt like I was living a dull life in black and white. Now that I am experiencing the poorest vision, I live my life in magnificent color because I fall deeper and deeper in love with my "Amla authentic self."

Reflection 363
Amla's Affirmation for All Beings
I am authentic, I am brave, and I am strong. With that, I am enough.

Reflection 364
From My Heart to Yours
The peace in me honors the peace in you.

Reflection 365
Amla Mehta's Sign-Off Signature Saying
Shine Love!
Shine Light!
Shine You!

About Amla Mehta

Amla is a speaker, teacher, and author who speaks and writes about living authentically, embodying self-love, and expressing your truth. As a legally blind woman, she is an advocate and activist on behalf of all people living with disabilities, whether they have mobility, hearing, vision, cognitive, or other challenges.

Amla graduated from the University of Connecticut with a degree in sociology. She has also developed her own intensive yoga and meditation practice, a discipline that she draws on for writing, speaking, and inspiring others. She loves hugging trees and practicing meditation by the Farmington River in Connecticut.

Amla is the author of three books, *Eye With a View* (Memoir/Self-Help), *The Ultimate Guide to Self-Healing Volume 3* (a collaborative book) and *Success in Any Season* (another collaborative book).

Feel free to contact Amla to be a keynote speaker at your next event, and purchase her books at www.amlaspeaks.com

Shine Love!

Shine Light!

Shine You!

Facebook @amlainspires

https://www.facebook.com/AmlaInspires

Twitter @amlainspires

https://twitter.com/AmlaInspires

Instagram @amlainspires

Youtube @amlainspires

https://www.youtube.com/channel/UCFlGFeIe9eaSy aWNpVZMVCg

Also by Amla Mehta

Also by Amla Mehta

About Green Heart Living

Green Heart Living's mission is to make the world a more loving and peaceful place, one person at a time. Green Heart Living Press publishes inspirational books and stories of transformation, making the world a more loving and peaceful place, one book at a time.

Whether you have an idea for an inspirational book and want support through the writing process, or your book is already written and you are looking for a publishing path, Green Heart Living can help you get your book out into the world.

You can meet Green Heart authors on the Green Heart Living YouTube channel and the Green Heart Living podcast.

www.greenheartliving.com

www.greenheartlivingpress.com

Green Heart Living Press Publications

Success in Any Season

Your Daily Dose of PositiviDee

Redefining Masculinity

Growing Smarter: Collaboration Secrets to Transform Your Income and Impact

Transformation 2020

Transformation 2020 Companion Journal

The Great Pause: Blessings & Wisdom from COVID-19

The Great Pause Journal

Love Notes: Daily Wisdom for the Soul

Green Your Heart, Green Your World